Tell Me More About Your Life!

Children's Ministry Curriculum

By Katy Collins and Stanley Scism

Introducing students of all
ages to major Bible
Characters—Genesis
through Revelation!

Wonderful Words

iUniverse, Inc.
New York   Bloomington

Tell Me More About Your Life!
Children's Ministry Curriculum

iUniverse books may be ordered through booksellers or by contacting:

iUniverse
1663 Liberty Drive
Bloomington, IN 47403
www.iuniverse.com
1-800-Authors (1-800-288-4677)

www.wonderfulwords.ws   Order from:
www.stanleyscism.com   USA: www.wonderfulwords.com
www.scismchristianuniversity.com India: Scism Christian Institute
                                        L-2 Green Park Main
                                        New Delhi 110016
                                        India

ISBN: 978-1-4401-7399-8 (sc)
ISBN: 978-1-4401-7400-1 (ebk)

Printed in the United States of America

iUniverse rev. date: 7/11/2010

Preface:

The vast majority of this text is by Katy Collins. I wrote the outline and a very few other things, including the interpretation of Judas Iscariot as being motivated by greed, and I reordered the lessons in chronological order (although scholars dispute Jonah's time).

I suggested the very general pacing to cover selected topics in a Biblical overview. Katy formatted the text to Biblical characters and wrote the structural format of individual lessons and the 'Overview of Lesson Parts.' I edited, but the thoughts are hers.

What can I say? She's a jewel.

The lessons provide stories and studies of Bible characters over one year, ideal for small Sunday schools where mixed-age groups gather, and for new groups of children coming to Jesus Christ.

Stanley Scism

Curriculum Goals: To...

1. Overview the Bible, investigate and explore different stories and parts of New and Old Testaments through eyes of new Biblical characters each week.
2. Provide a single-lesson framework easily adjusted to different age levels and group sizes, using no outside materials.
3. Simultaneously teach and reinforce different Christian living concepts: Bible study, memorization, praise and worship, prayer.
4. Promote active involvement in God's Word through discussing, questioning, acting.
5. Invite children to personal salvation in Jesus by making God's Word meaningful, real, and exciting.

Table of Contents

Overview of the Lesson Parts

Take Roll/Memory Verse:

Goal: Start class in an organized manner.

Settle everyone in the children's ministry area. Take roll, hear older kids' memory verses. Let children socialize and play. (Note: Most children age 7 and up can memorize Scripture. Don't try to make kids too young memorize Scripture. Reward students for memory verse work, don't punish them for not doing it. For example, keep track of who memorizes Scripture each week, then, on a rest week, award those who completed a certain amount of Scripture memorization.)

Sing/Movement:

Goal: Teach children to worship and praise God.

Teachers lead songs, as often as possible, with actions and movement. Duration depends on students' age group. Pull older students up front to help lead actions. Instruments, if available, help. If you have extras, pass them to children to involve them. Consider songs teaching Bible facts, like a song listing Bible books or the Ten Commands.

Teach the Lesson:

Goal: Teach children to study Scripture

Creatively always start by quickly reviewing last week's lesson. Avoid reading students a lesson—to help students connect with the Bible character, present material in a more interesting way, such as (and these are only a few):

1. *Act it out:* Write scripts for older students to read and act. Give it to them a week ahead, so they can practice and become familiar with it.
2. *Read it like a story:* Write the lesson into a story format with dialogue. Read it to students using different voices and actions.
3. *Use characters:* Cut out characters from felt, paper, or fabric. Design a background to act the story out on (a white sheet works well for this). Pull kids up front to move the characters as you read the story.
4. *Mime:* Pull kids up front to be characters as you read the part. You tell the story, and they do what the story character does (For instance, pretending to be Moses' mother, bending down to put the basket in the river).
5. *Draw as you go:* If you have a white board or chalk board, draw characters and background as you tell the story.
6. *Use various props:* Anything you can find that resembles part of the story helps you teach. For example, when telling the story of Adam and Eve in the garden, a piece of fruit shows as an example of what Eve ate.
7. *Move the lesson to a new location:* If you are in a church building, move outdoors or elsewhere near the building. This can help teach stories like Creation, so students can look at plants, animals, the sun.

8. *Invite guests:* Have guest teachers help act out stories. Usually the youth group happily contributes members to help younger kids.

9. *Make puppets:* You can make Bible story characters from different materials, for instance, decorate the ends of socks with faces and put your hand in them to make them 'talk'. Sticks, cardboard, and other supplies also work. After you make a set of male and female puppets of different ages, you can act out almost any Bible story with the same set. A table with a cloth over it can hide students as they act with puppets.

10. *Take a mental trip:* Have children shut their eyes and visualize the story as you tell it descriptively. Then have students tell what they 'saw' in their imaginations.

11. *Interview a character:* Have someone (adult, youth or older child) pretend to be the Bible character, dress up and/or talk differently than usual, introduce him/herself, tell about his/her life. Children can ask the character questions about life in Bible times.

12. *Make a timeline of the story together:* On the white board, chalkboard, or on paper, you and the students can draw/write the events in the story in order.

Leading Discussion:

Goal: Reinforce Bible lessons, teach children to draw life applications from the Bible

Leading discussion demands students think about it, so can benefit students most of all. Start with *knowledge questions* to make sure they understand the story and process of events. Have students think through what happened in sequence. Move to *understanding questions* to make them think about who characters were, why they acted as they did, what God thought of them. Last, ask *life application questions* to make students apply lessons to their own lives. Instead of trying to get through the most questions possible, make discussion meaningful and deep. Focus on quality, not quantity, of answers. Follow a question with more questions if students get the answer wrong or could add more information.

Knowledge Questions:

- What happened first in this story?
- What happened second, third, fourth...?
- Where did this story take place?
- Who were the main characters?
- When did the story take place?
- How would you describe the main character?
- Who were some of the other characters?
- Summarize the story in your own words.

Understanding Questions:

- What would you ask these people if they were here right now?
- Why do you think they did what they did?
- How do you think God felt about their lives? Why?
- Why do you think their life stories was included in the Bible?
- What about their lives do you think they would be most proud or most ashamed of?
- What made these people special?

Life Application Questions:

- What can we learn from their lives?
- Would you like to have lived around them? Why or why not?
- Do you think these people would be good friends? Why or why not?

- What lesson from their experiences can you apply to your life?
- What did you learn that you could share with others?

Leading Prayer:

Goals: To unite in prayer together and to teach children to pray.

Begin prayer time by talking about prayer focus. Next, lead children through each part of prayer's process: praise, repent, ask for others, and ask for ourselves. This cycle teaches kids to talk to God in a simple, easily remembered way. You (or they) can expand the cycle to lengthen prayer time when they are ready to pray independently. At the end of prayer time, ask the students for prayer requests. Encourage them to pray for their families, friends and communities. They can start praying at a very young age.

Closing:

Goals: Review lessons and check for understanding.

Use closing to summarize the entire lesson. Quickly review the character you studied. Ask students questions to determine what they learned. Preview who they'll study during the next week.

Extra Time:

If you have extra time:

1. Pick another method to teach that you did not use, teach the lesson again in a different way.
2. Let students become teachers and you become the student. Let them teach you the lesson.
3. Learn new songs or invent actions to a song you already know.

4. Play a game—for example, a 'sword' drill where students try to be the first to locate a Bible verse.
5. Practice a program for one of the "Rest Weeks". The students can practice each week for a special program to put on for the church.

Rest Week Ideas:

Rest weeks are designed to allow for other church events, or, in the absence of those, to give the teacher and students a break from normal routine. Try some of these ideas during the year.

1. Present a program for the church. Programs could be singing, skits, plays, or combine anything students invent.
2. Celebrate! Invite children to bring food and special treats. Play games and enjoy each other's company.
3. Take a trip. Walk to a special location in your area, like a river or a building. Enjoy time together.
4. Stage an awards ceremony for your memory verse winners.
5. Have a costume party, when students dress up as their favorite Bible character they've studied so far.

One Hour Schedule for Various Age Groups:

If you have many teachers and a variety of age groups, you may want to split the Sunday School into age groups. Suggested schedule adjustments for various age groups:

> With younger kids, minimize the time they spend sitting and listening, let them move as much as possible. With older kids, extend lessons with discussions.

Of course, in a small group, work with the schedule to make it work for all ages simultaneously.

Ages 2-5

Take roll/Socialize: 10 minutes
Sing/Movement: 20 minutes
Bible Story: 10 minutes
Discussion: 5 minutes
Game/Play time/Sing: 10 minutes
Prayer/Closing: 5 minutes

Ages 6-9

Take roll/Socialize/Memory Verse: 10 minutes
Sing/Movement: 15 minutes
Bible Story: 10 minutes
Discussion: 10 minutes
Prayer: 10 minutes
Closing: 5 minutes

Ages 10-13

Take roll/Socialize/Memory Verse: 10 minutes
Sing/movement: 10 minutes
Bible Story: 20 minutes
Discussion: 10 minutes
Prayer: 10 minutes
Closing: 5 minutes

Lesson 1

Biblical Character: God
Scripture Text: Genesis 1-2
Memory Verse: Genesis 1:1
Lesson Outline:
- *Background* – The earth had no form, was blank, waiting for a Creator to make it into something.
- *Story* – God created the whole world in 7 days. On the first day, he separated light from darkness. One the second day, he created the sky. On the third day, he made land and plants; on the fourth day, the sun, moon, and stars; on the fifth day, fish and birds; on the sixth day, land animals and man. On the seventh day of creation, he rested from his work. He called everything he made 'good.'
- *Main Achievement* - He created everything that we see around us in one week.
- *Good/Bad Character Traits* – God displayed love, care, and intelligence in creating the world.

Prayer Focus: Respect for God's creation
- *Praise* – Thank God for creating the earth, animals, and people.
- *Repent* – I'm sorry we don't love and respect your creation all the time.
- *Ask for Others* – Let everyone realize you are the true Creator and God.
- *Ourselves* – Help us to be more thankful and more respectful of your creation (earth, animals, and people).

Lesson 2

Biblical Characters: Adam and Eve
Scripture Text: Genesis 3-4
Memory Verse: Genesis 3:15
Lesson Outline:

- *Background* – Adam and Eve were created on the sixth day of creation. God made Eve out of Adam's side. They lived together in Eden's garden in perfection—no sin, disease or death. God told them they could eat from any tree in the garden except the Tree of Knowing Good and Evil. If they ate from that tree, they'd die.
- *Story* – One day Eve was in the garden looking at the forbidden tree. The devil, in the form of a snake, came to her and tempted her to eat of the tree. When she did, she died spiritually and was doomed to die physically. She then convinced Adam to eat, too. Then God made them leave the garden, but God planned to restore them through Jesus' sacrifice on the cross.
- *Main Achievement* - They later became the parents of the whole human race. Everyone, including the Messiah, came from them.
- *Good/Bad Character Traits* – Good: they wanted to walk with God and have a personal relationship with him. Bad: they allowed themselves to be drawn away from God by their own hunger for knowledge and power.

Prayer Focus: Sin

- *Praise* – Thank Jesus for being merciful to the sinful human race by coming to earth to die for our sins.
- *Repent* – We're sorry that we are sinful people.
- *Ask for Others* – Let everyone know about and be sorry for their sins and realize they need God.
- *Ourselves* – Help us to always be sorry for our sins, so we can be more like you.

Lesson 3

Biblical Character: Noah
Scripture Text: Genesis 6-9
Memory Verse: Genesis 6:8
Lesson Outline:

- *Background* – The whole world became so sinful and bad God decided to completely destroy it with a flood. He was going to kill everything and start again.
- *Story* – God noticed one man, Noah, was righteous, so decided to give Noah and his family a chance to be saved. He told Noah to build a big ship called an ark. All around Noah, people made fun of him, but he built the ark anyway. God also told Noah to take 2 of every kind of animal with him into the ark. When rain began, only people in the ark lived. It rained 40 days and 40 nights. Finally, the earth dried up, so eight people and all the animals could leave the ark and start their lives over again.
- *Main Achievement* – When God told him to build an ark, he obeyed God and saved his family and all the world's animals.
- *Good/Bad Character Traits* – Noah was righteous when the whole world was sinful, and he was willing to obey a command he did not understand (the earth never had rain before).

Prayer Focus: Salvation of Humans

- *Praise* – We're thankful you cared enough for humans to save them from the flood.
- *Repent* – We're sorry we continue to sin, even though you died to save us.
- *Ask for Others* – Help people realize Jesus is the way of salvation before it is too late, as it was in Noah's time.
- *Ourselves* – Give us a desire to be saved and follow Jesus.

Lesson 4

Biblical Character: Job
Scripture Text: Job 1-3, 41-42
Memory Verse: Job 13:15
Lesson Outline:

- *Background* – Job was a faithful and godly man, also blessed by God with his family and possessions.
- *Story* – One day God asked Satan if he noticed his faithful servant Job. Satan said Job would not be so faithful if God took away all blessings. God allowed Satan to touch Job's possessions—all Job's children and cattle died, and his home and barns burned. He had nothing, but still served God. Satan then asked for permission to make Job sick, believing Job would curse God if he was bodily miserable. Still Job did not curse God, but trusted. Even though his wife and friends told him that he'd be better off dead, still he blessed God. In the end, because of Job's faithfulness, God blessed him with more children and possessions than he had before.
- *Main Achievement* - Job stood strong through Satan's severe trials.
- *Good/Bad Character Traits* – Job was faithful in the most difficult trails humans ever face.

Prayer Focus: Trust in hard times

- *Praise* – Thank you for never leaving or forsaking us.
- *Repent* – We're sorry we have bad attitudes when things in our lives don't go well.
- *Ask for Others* – Let our ability to stand strong in hard times witness to our family and friends.
- *Ourselves* – Give us strength to trust in you always, during good and bad times.

Lesson 5

Biblical Characters: Abraham and Sarah
Scripture Text: Genesis 12-22
Memory Verse: Genesis 12:3
Lesson Outline:

- *Background* – Abraham lived in a sinful land. God told him to get up and leave. Abraham left his familiar country and went to a strange land where he knew no one.
- *Story* – God saw Abraham's obedience, and it made him happy, so God gave Abraham and his wife a promise to make them a great nation of people. Sarah and Abraham could not have children and they were very old. Many years later, though, finally their son Isaac was born.
- *Main Achievement* - Abraham had faith in God, even when circumstances seemed very bad, and God's promises hadn't been fulfilled yet.
- *Good/Bad Character Traits* – Abraham had great faith, but sometimes doubted that God could do what he promised.

Prayer Focus: Promises of God

- *Praise* – We are so thankful you keep all your promises you make to people.
- *Repent* – We're sorry that sometimes we break our promises.
- *Ask for Others* – Help all humans follow you and claim your promise of eternal life for themselves.
- *Ourselves* – Help us be more faithful keeping our promises and trusting you when you promise to us.

Lesson 6

Biblical Character: Jacob
Scripture Text: Genesis 27-32
Memory Verse: Genesis 32:28
Lesson Outline:

- *Background* – Jacob was Esau's twin brother. Jacob and Esau did not get along. Esau was older, so he was promised their father's birthright and blessing. Jacob wanted these very badly, so he and his mother Rebecca planned to steal them from Esau.
- *Story* – One day Esau came back from hunting, very hungry. Jacob was cooking lentils, and Esau asked for some food. Jacob told him he could have it if he would pay him the birthright. Esau agreed. To get the blessing, Rebecca helped him—Isaac was going blind, so they dressed up Jacob in Esau's clothes, brought food like Esau's, and tricked Isaac. This made Esau very angry, so Jacob ran away.
- *Main Achievement* - Jacob later became the father of Israel's 12 tribes. God changed his name to Israel and blessed him.
- *Good/Bad Character Traits* – Bad: Jacob deceived and tricked people to get what he wanted. Good: he served God and was obedient later in life.

Prayer Focus: Serving God
- *Praise* – Thank you for choosing us and letting us become your children.
- *Repent* – We're sorry we sometimes don't have a sincere desire to serve you.
- *Ask for Others* – Give our community's, the the whole world's, people a desire to serve you.
- *Ourselves* – Help us be faithful to your commands and love you with all our hearts.

Lesson 7

Biblical Character: Joseph
Scripture Text: Genesis 37-49
Memory Verse: Genesis 46:3
Lesson Outline:

- *Background* – Joseph was one of Jacob's sons. His father liked him best of his children, so he made Joseph a special multi-colored coat. So his brothers hated him.
- *Story* – One night Joseph had two dreams about his family bowing down to serve him. He told his family about the dreams and they all got angry. One day Joseph went looking for his brothers. When they saw him coming, they planned to get rid of him. Some wanted to kill him, but Judah convinced them to sell Joseph to some travelers instead. The travelers took him to Egypt to sell him. Joseph's brothers took his special coat, smeared it with blood and lied to their father, saying an animal had eaten Joseph.
- *Main Achievement* - Later, after many years in Egypt, Joseph saved his whole family and all Egypt from a terrible famine.
- *Good/Bad Character Traits* – Bad: Joseph had pride when he was young. Good: he later served God with patience through many hard years in Egypt.

Prayer Focus: Deliverance out of problems

- *Praise* – Thank you that you deliver us from trouble.
- *Repent* – Forgive us for not always trusting you to take care of our problems.
- *Ask for Others* – Help this world's people to know you alone can solve all their problems.
- *Ourselves* – Help us trust you more, even when it appears the situation won't work out.

Lesson 8

Biblical Character: Miriam
Scripture Text: Exodus 1-2
Memory Verse: Exodus 2:25
Lesson Outline:

- *Background* – After living in peace with the Egyptians for many years, the Hebrews were enslaved by Pharaoh (Egypt's king). Hebrews got so strong that Egyptians had to find a way to keep them under control, so they ordered all baby boys killed at birth.
- *Story* – Moses was born to a Levite family. When they saw what a good child he was, they hid him for 3 months so he wouldn't be killed. After 3 months, his mother couldn't hide him any longer, so she made a small boat from a basket. She put him in it and floated him downriver towards the Pharaoh's house. Moses' sister Miriam followed to see what happened. The basket floated right up to Pharoah's daughter. She recognized he was a Hebrew, but wanted to save him. She named him Moses and asked Miriam to take him to someone to nurse him. Miriam took him back to her mother and they raised him until he was old enough to go back to Pharaoh's home.
- *Main Achievement* - She quickly thought of a way to get Moses back to her family, and saved his life.
- *Good/Bad Character Traits* – Good: Miriam was very brave and smart. Bad: sometimes she was a bit proud later in life.

Prayer Focus: Faith

- *Praise* – Thank you that you always provide our problems' perfect solutions.
- *Repent* – We're sorry we sometimes don't have enough faith to believe you can take care of our problems.
- *Ask for Others* – Increase our church's faith.
- *Ourselves* – Give us faith to believe you can do anything and use anyone.

Lesson 9

Biblical Character: Pharaoh
Scripture Text: Exodus 3-15
Memory Verse: Exodus 12:13
Lesson Outline:

- *Background* – Pharaoh was king in Egypt. He ruled the whole country and used the Hebrews as slaves.
- *Story* – One day Moses came and demanded he release Hebrews from slavery. Pharaoh refused and actually made Hebrews' jobs harder. Moses came back over and over to Pharaoh asking him to release Hebrews. God sent plagues to the Egypt to force them to release Hebrews. Pharaoh kept refusing. Finally, God sent a death-plague on all Egypt's firstborn sons. This convinced Pharaoh to let Hebrews go, and they escaped into the wilderness. Egyptians came after them, but God rescued Hebrews through the Red Sea by parting the waters, meanwhile killing all Egyptians chasing them.
- *Main Achievement* - Pharaoh was used by God to free Hebrews and to prove to the unbelievers there's only One True God.
- *Good/Bad Character Traits* – Pharaoh had many bad character traits. He was proud and mean to Hebrew slaves. He refused to humble himself until God forced him.

Prayer Focus: Power of God

- *Praise* – We're thankful you have power over all kings and nations.
- *Repent* – We're sorry we sometimes harden our hearts to your love and power, as Pharaoh did.
- *Ask for Others* – Do signs and wonders today so people know you are the true God.
- *Ourselves* – Through your power, use us to speak to unbelievers as you used Moses.

Lesson 10

Biblical Character: Moses
Scripture Text: Exodus 15-20
Memory Verse: Exodus 20:2-3
Lesson Outline:

- *Background* – God used Moses to deliver Israel out of Egypt. He became their leader and led them across the Red Sea.
- *Story* – God wants to give his people laws to live by, to teach them how to worship, what was right and wrong, and how to run their community. God called Moses to the top of a high mountain called Sinai to give him the Laws, including the Ten Commands.
- *Main Achievement* - Moses' strong leadership led his people out of slavery.
- *Good/Bad Character Traits* – Good: Moses very faithfully served and trusted God. Bad: he also had a temper that kept him from entering the Promised Land.

Prayer Focus: God can use anyone

- *Praise* – We praise you that you can use anyone to accomplish your will.
- *Repent* – We're sorry we sometimes don't do what you tell us.
- *Ask for Others* – Let people's hearts around us to be tender to your loving message.
- *Ourselves* – Help us do things for you that we're scared to do.

Lesson 11

Biblical Character: Aaron
Scripture Text: Exodus 32
Memory Verse: Deuteronomy 6:4
Lesson Outline:

- *Background* – Aaron was Moses' older brother. He was part of a group of Hebrews delivered from Egypt.
- *Story* – Moses was on the mountain getting the Ten Commands, and Aaron was left in charge of the people. Moses was so long returning that the people got impatient and demanded Aaron make other gods for them to follow. Aaron took their jewelry and other gold and sculpted a golden calf for people to worship. He told them this was their god, and declared a feast day to it. When Moses finally came down the mountain, God punished the people for disobedience. They learned there was only one true God.
- *Main Achievement* - Even though Aaron was disobeyed God, God still made him Israel's first priest.
- *Good/Bad Character Traits* – Bad: Aaron weakly, mistakenly caved in to people's demands. Good: Later, Aaron proved himself very dedicated in priesthood to God.

Prayer Focus: The Salvation of God

- *Praise* – We're thankful you provided a way for us to get close to you, though the ultimate sacrifice of your body on the cross.
- *Repent* – Forgive us we sometimes forget what you did for us.
- *Ask for Others* – Help us draw this world to your love.
- *Ourselves* – Help us to be holy like you, through Jesus' blood.

Lesson 12

Biblical Character: Rahab
Scripture Text: Joshua 1-10
Memory Verse: Joshua 2:11
Lesson Outline:
- *Background* – Rahab was born in the sinful city of Jericho. She lived as a prostitute. Her house was on the city wall.
- *Story* – One day two Israelite spies came to the city in disguise to see if Israel could defeat Jericho. Rahab took them in, protected them from the king, told them the good news that everyone in the city was terrified of the Hebrews' God. She made them promise they would not kill her or her family when they destroyed the city. They told her to hang a red thread in her window. Anyone in that house would not be killed. She saved them from Jericho's soldiers by letting them over wall's edge. When they came back with the army, they protected her and her family by the red thread. They later joined the Hebrew family.
- *Main Achievement* - She assisted the spies and helped Hebrews destroy Jericho.
- *Good/Bad Character Traits* – Bad: She had been a prostitute and didn't know the true God. Good: she had very strong faith and trust in Israel's God.

Prayer Focus: The Family of God
- *Praise* – Thank you for letting us to be part of your family, even though we don't deserve it.
- *Repent* – Forgive us we sometimes forget how merciful you are.
- *Ask for Others* – Draw more people into your family so they can live for you.
- *Ourselves* – Let us be unify in your love, like a real family.

Lesson 13

REST

Lesson 14

Biblical Character: Samson
Scripture Text: Judges 13-16
Memory Verse: Judges 16:28
Lesson Outline:
- *Background* – God chose and made special plans for Samson even before his birth. He was a Nazarite and couldn't drink or cut his hair. God told his mother he'd use Samson to deliver Israel from the Philistines.
- *Story* – Samson had a hard time being faithful to his calling. He fell in love with a girl, Delilah, who deceived him into telling the secret of his strength with God: his uncut hair. While he was sleeping, she cut his hair and called Philistines to come and capture him. They took him, put out his eyes. Later, after his hair grew back, Philistines called him to come to a party so they could make fun of him. God granted him strength, he shook the pillars of the temple and killed 3,000 people when he died.
- *Main Achievement* - He killed more people while dying than he did while living.
- *Good/Bad Character Traits* – Bad: Samson had a very hard time being faithful to his calling. Good: at the end of his life, he came back to God in humility.

Prayer Focus: Witnessing
- *Praise* – Thank you for using people who have sinned, to do great work for you.
- *Repent* – We're sorry we sin and sometimes disappoint you.
- *Ask for Others* – Let our families' and friends' hearts be tender toward you.
- *Ourselves* - Help us witness boldly.

Lesson 15

Biblical Character: Hannah
Scripture Text: I Samuel 1-2
Memory Verse: I Samuel 1:17
Lesson Outline:

- *Background* – Hannah was the wife of a good man, but the man's other wife had children and Hannah didn't. The other wife kept teasing her, so she wanted a child.
- *Story* – One day Hannah prayed and prayed to God for a child until she was lying on the ground and only her lips moved, with no sound coming out. She promised God if she had a son, she would dedicate the son to him. While she lay on the temple floor, the priest Eli came by and accused her of being drunk. She told him she had poured out her soul to God, and he blessed her. Later, God granted her the son she prayed for, and the son became an influential prophet of Israel.
- *Main Achievement* - She was the mother of a man God used to bring people back to him.
- *Good/Bad Character Traits* – Hannah had a spirit of sacrifice. She did not claim God's blessings as her own, but gave them back to him.

Prayer Focus: God answers prayer

- *Praise* – Thank you that you always answer our prayers.
- *Repent* – We're sorry we sometimes don't pray as much as we should.
- *Ask for Others* – Give unbelievers a desire to serve you and sacrifice their lives for you.
- *Ourselves* – Give us a hunger to pray.

Lesson 16

Biblical Character: Saul
Scripture Text: I Samuel 8-16
Memory Verse: I Samuel 15:22
Lesson Outline:

- *Background* – Saul was anointed as Israel's first king by the prophet Samuel.
- *Story* – Once Saul and his army went to conquer people. Before Saul left, Samuel told him to not let any animal or person in the city live, but to kill everything. When God gave victory, Saul thought maybe he could take back some cattle to sacrifice to God. When Samuel saw this, he was angry, and told Saul he should obey God's command rather than doing what he wanted. Even though sacrificing pleased God, God wants obedience to His commands most of all.
- *Main Achievement* - Saul was Israel's first king.
- *Good/Bad Character Traits* – Good: Saul wanted to serve God. Bad: He let his pride interfere with his obedience. He thought he knew better than God.

Prayer Focus: Obedience

- *Praise* – Thank you, Lord, that you instruct us when we're wrong.
- *Repent* – Forgive us for not always obeying your command.
- *Ask for Others* - Help the world see that obeying your commands brings blessing.
- *Ourselves* – Remind us that serving you is a privilege.

Lesson 17

Biblical Character: Goliath
Scripture Text: I Samuel 17
Memory Verse: I Samuel 17:45
Lesson Outline:
- *Background* – Goliath was the Philistine army's most powerful warrior, and a giant. No one else could carry his heavy armor. He always yelled threats at Israel's army. No one could fight him, because he was so much stronger than anyone they had.
- *Story* – A young shepherd boy named David delivered lunch to his brothers on the battlefield, heard what Goliath said to the Hebrew army, and wanted to go and fight Goliath. Everyone laughed when he went to fight the giant with only a slingshot and a few stones, but with God's help, he could kill the giant. He ran and cut off the giant's head.
- *Main Achievement* - Goliath was a great warrior for the Philistine army.
- *Good/Bad Character Traits* – Goliath was proud. He did not believe in the true God, only in his own strength.

Prayer Focus: Strength and trust
- *Praise* – Thank you that with your Name, we can't fail.
- *Repent* – We are sorry we sometimes we don't trust you like we should.
- *Ask for Others* – Let this whole world see that you are the one true God.
- *Ourselves* – Help us trust you even when we are afraid of what might happen to us.

Lesson 18

Biblical Character: Jonathan
Scripture Text: I Samuel 20
Memory Verse: I Samuel 20:17
Lesson Outline:

- *Background* – Jonathan, Saul's son, befriended David, who was anointed as Israel's new king.
- *Story* – Saul tried to kill David. When he told Jonathan this, Jonathan warned David, allowing David to escape from Saul and live.
- *Main Achievement* - He helped the new king, David, escape from the old king, Saul.
- *Good/Bad Character Traits* – Jonathan loyally befriended David even though it meant betraying his father.

Prayer Focus: Friendship

- *Praise* – Thank you for good friends who love us.
- *Repent* – We're sorry we sometimes don't act lovingly towards our friends.
- *Ask for Others* – Help other people be drawn to you through our love and friendship
- *Ourselves* – Give us love for each other.

Lesson 19

Biblical Character: David
Scripture Text: Psalms 23; 27, 150
Memory Verse: Psalm 23:1
Lesson Outline:

- *Background* – David started small. He was the youngest brothers, every day he watched flocks.
- *Story* - During that time in his life, he didn't get much respect, but he still served God faithfully. He cared for the sheep even when a lion or bear would attack. David knew how to praise God in all circumstances: fear, disappointment, repentance, shame, and joy. Because of his devotion and worship, he was called a man after God's own heart. God listened to David because of his praise.
- *Main Achievement* - David was a successful king and wrote most of the Psalms.
- *Good/Bad Character Traits* – David was humble before God and people, even though he had a high position.

Prayer Focus: Praise and Worship

- *Praise* – Thank you for examples of praise and worship in the Bible.
- *Repent* – We're sorry we sometimes don't praise and worship you with our whole hearts.
- *Ask for Others* – Let everyone in this world realize they need to praise the one, true God.
- *Ourselves* – Give us hearts of worship like David, and let our lives be lights of praise.

Lesson 20

Biblical Character: Solomon
Scripture Text: I Kings 3
Memory Verse: I Kings 3:11
Lesson Outline:

- *Background* – Solomon was Israel's third king. His major goal as king was to build a temple to God.
- *Story* – When Solomon was anointed King, God came to him in a dream and asked him what he could give him. Solomon asked God for wisdom to judge his people and to tell the difference between right and wrong. This pleased God so much that he gave him long life, riches, honor, and promised Solomon would be the wisest king to ever live.
- *Main Achievement* - Solomon wrote several Bible books: Proverbs, Ecclesiastes, and Song of Songs.
- *Good/Bad Character Traits* – Good: Solomon was a wise, godly man. Bad: later in life he was drifted from God due to his pagan wives.

Prayer Focus: Wisdom

- *Praise* – Thank you for wisdom you gave us through King Solomon.
- *Repent* – Forgive us for ignoring what you told us.
- *Ask for Others* – Help others see that following you is a wise decision.
- *Ourselves* – Give us desire to understand your wisdom and practice it.

Lesson 21

Biblical Character: Jonah
Scripture Text: Jonah 1-4
Memory Verse: Jonah 2:9
Lesson Outline:
- *Background* – Jonah prophesied for God. God called Jonah to preach to Nineveh, but Jonah didn't want to go because it was such a bad place. He tried to go another way, but God stopped his ship with a storm.
- *Story* – The storm was so bad that men on ship cast lots to tell who had angered the gods. The lot fell to Jonah. He confessed and told them to throw him into the ocean so they would live and only he would die. God sent a huge fish to swallow up Jonah and protect him. Inside it, Jonah repented and told God he'd go preach to Nineveh. After 3 days, the fish spit out Jonah on dry ground. Jonah went and preached repentance to the city. They turned to God.
- *Main Achievement* - God used Jonah to get Nineveh to turn back to him in repentance.
- *Good/Bad Character Traits* – Jonah very stubbornly did not want to obey God when told what to do.

Prayer Focus: God corrects us like a Father.
- *Praise* – Thank you for being able to correct us when we go wrong.
- *Repent* – Forgive our sometimes not following your perfect plan.
- *Ask for Others* – Lovingly correct our friends and family who don't serve you.
- *Ourselves* – Help us humbly accept your correction when we mess up.

Lesson 22

Biblical Character: Elijah
Scripture Text: I Kings 17-19
Memory Verse: I Kings 18:37
Lesson Outline:
- *Background* – Elijah was a prophet of God used by God to do many miracles.
- *Story* – One day Elijah challenged King Ahab's prophets to a contest to see which of their 'gods' would answer with fire. Baal's prophets put a bull on the altar, danced and cut themselves, but got no answer. Next, Elijah built an altar and poured water over his sacrifice, so the fire could not be lit by human hands. He prayed to God asking for fire. God answered, and fire consumed the sacrifice.
- *Main Achievement* - Elijah did not die; God took him to heaven in a whirlwind.
- *Good/Bad Character Traits* – Good: Elijah was a loyal, bold man of God. Bad: he sometimes got discouraged and depressed.

Prayer Focus: God provides everything
- *Praise* – Thank you for caring for us when we don't have food or shelter.
- *Repent* – We're sorry we sometimes don't trust you to supply our needs.
- *Ask for Others* – Help the world's people have enough food and other things they need to live.
- *Ourselves* – Keep us safe and provide for all our church's and families' needs.

Lesson 23

Biblical Character: Elisha
Scripture Text: 2 Kings 1-8
Memory Verse: 2 Kings 2:9
Lesson Outline:

- *Background* – Elisha as a young man decided to follow prophet Elijah. Elijah knew the Lord was going to take him to heaven.
- *Story* – On the day Elijah was going to be taken to heaven, he told Elisha to leave him so he could go to Jordan River. Elisha refused to leave. Elijah struck the river water, which parted so the two men could cross. Elijah asked Elisha what he could do for him before he was taken away. Elisha asked for a double portion of Elijah's anointing. Elijah said that if he saw Elijah as he was taken away, Elisha would receive his request. Elisha saw him be taken, and picked up Elijah's mantle when it fell to the ground. Then he went to the Jordan and asked where the God of Elijah was. He hit the water as Elijah had, and the waters parted. This let him know he would have a ministry twice as fruitful as Elijah's.
- *Main Achievement* - Elisha persevered and received the anointing he desired.
- *Good/Bad Character Traits* – Elisha faithfully persevered even when Elijah discouraged him. He refused to be turned away from his desire to receive anointed ministry.

Prayer Focus: Serving God

- *Praise* – Thank you that you answer our prayers to grow closer to you.
- *Repent* – We're sorry we sometimes don't desire things you want us to.
- *Ask for Others* – Help the world be drawn to your power and salvation.
- *Ourselves* – Give us a desire to serve you with all our hearts.

Lesson 24

Biblical Character: Isaiah
Scripture Text: Isaiah 6, 7, 53
Memory Verse: Isaiah 6:8
Lesson Outline:
- *Background* – Isaiah lived in Jerusalem his whole life. His ministry lasted 50 years during a time of great prosperity and success.
- *Story* – God used Isaiah to bring a message of repentance to his wealthy generation. He told them to abandon worldly things and turn to God, who loved them. God also spoke through Isaiah to his people the prophecy of the Messiah's coming. His prophecies give us a good picture of the man Jesus would be. In the New Testament, we see all these prophecies fulfilled by Jesus Christ—impossible without God's inspiration!
- *Main Achievement* - Isaiah left a legacy of prophecy and encouragement in his book.
- *Good/Bad Character Traits* – Isaiah spoke boldly and faithfully for God, even when it made him unpopular.

Prayer Focus: Inspiration from God's Word
- *Praise* – Thank you for your inspiring words to us in the Bible.
- *Repent* – Forgive us when we don't always trust your Word.
- *Ask for Others* – Let your Word go to the entire world to draw people to salvation.
- *Ourselves* – Let us be inspired by the Bible and your communication with us.

Lesson 25

Biblical Character: Jeremiah
Scripture Text: Jeremiah 1
Memory Verse: Jeremiah 1:5
Lesson Outline:

- *Background* –Jeremiah was born in a priestly family and a godly home.
- *Story* – God started speaking to Jeremiah one day, telling him God had chosen him to prophesy to nations. God said he'd picked Jeremiah specifically when Jeremiah was still in his mother's stomach, not even formed yet. Jeremiah replied that he couldn't do it, said he still spoke like a child. God promised to be with him wherever he went and help him. Then God touched Jeremiah's mouth and told him God would put his own words in Jeremiah's mouth.
- *Main Achievement* - Jeremiah left behind an inspired book of prophecy encouraging believers.
- *Good/Bad Character Traits* –
- Bad: Jeremiah did not have confidence at first. Good: after God touched him, he trusted God to help him.

Prayer Focus: God made us.

- *Praise* – Thank you, Jesus, that you made us and know exactly who and what we are.
- *Repent* – Forgive us for not always going to you first with our problems.
- *Ask for Others* – Help our school friends to understand Jesus made and loves them.
- *Ourselves* – Give us faith to trust you more.

Lesson 26

REST

Lesson 27

Biblical Character: Shadrach, Meshach, Abednego
Scripture Text: Daniel 3
Memory Verse: Daniel 3:17
Lesson Outline:

- *Background* – Shadrach, Meshach, and Abednego were three young men forced to serve in the Babylonian king's palace.
- *Story* – A law said everyone in the palace had to bow down and worship an idol. When the 3 young men refused, they were brought to the king. He ordered them thrown into a fiery furnace to be killed. They told him God could deliver them, but that even if he chose not to, they still wouldn't worship idols. They were thrown into fire so hot it killed them men who forced them in. After a few minutes, the king looked in the furnace and saw 4 people, even though only 3 had been thrown in. They opened the door to let the 3 young men out, since the one true God had protected them.
- *Main Achievement* - The young men proved to pagans the one true God by standing up for their faith.
- *Good/Bad Character Traits* – The Hebrew boys had great faith in God's ability to protect them.

Prayer Focus: Standing up for Jesus

- *Praise* – Thank you for backing us up when we stand for you.
- *Repent* – Forgive us that sometimes we fear to testify about you.
- *Ask for Others* – Give everyone in our church trust to believe you can take care of us.
- *Ourselves* – Give us boldness to stand up for you when we are criticized.

Lesson 28

Biblical Character: Daniel
Scripture Text: Daniel 1-6
Memory Verse: Daniel 6:26
Lesson Outline:

- *Background* – Daniel was a servant in the household of a pagan king.
- *Story* – Some officials coaxed a king to pass a law that no one could worship anyone except the king. Daniel was brought before the king for worshiping the one true God. Even though the king liked Daniel, because of the law Daniel was thrown into a lion's den. During the night, God shut the lions' mouths so that they could not eat Daniel. When morning came, the king came to check to see if Daniel had survived. Daniel called back to him from the den that he was okay, that God had preformed a miracle for him. The king then realized Daniel served the one true God.
- *Main Achievement* - Daniel later received prophecy from God about the world's end.
- *Good/Bad Character Traits* – Daniel was faithful and true to God, even when opposed by someone very powerful.

Prayer Focus: Revelation of the True God

- *Praise* – We praise you for revealing your oneness to us.
- *Repent* – We repent we sometimes don't appreciate what you've done for us.
- *Ask for Others* – Reveal Jesus' oneness to everyone in the world.
- *Ourselves* – Give us better understanding of who you are.

Lesson 29

Biblical Character: Esther
Scripture Text: Esther 1-10
Memory Verse: Esther 4:14
Lesson Outline:

- *Background* – Esther was taken from her home to live in the palace of the king as a concubine. She eventually pleased the king so much he made her queen. She did not tell anyone at the palace that she was a Jew.
- *Story* – A man named Haman hated Jews. He decided to destroy them, and had the king decree that all Jews should be killed on a certain day. When Esther heard about this, she was very sad for her people. She fasted and prayed for God to help her, then prepared herself to go talk to the king. She went into the king's presence without an invitation, which was dangerous. The king, though, asked her what she wanted. Esther invited him and Haman to a special banquet. After 3 nights of banqueting, Esther asked the king for mercy for her people and revealed Haman as the man behind the evil plan. Haman was hanged, and Jews were saved by Esther's bravery.
- *Main Achievement* - Esther saved her people from death.
- *Good/Bad Character Traits* – Esther bravely risked her life for her people.

Prayer Focus: Boldness

- *Praise* – Thank you for taking care of your people.
- *Repent* – Forgive us we sometimes forget you love us and care for us.
- *Ask for Others* – Let our church's bold testimonies draw others to salvation.
- *Ourselves* – Give us boldness to talk about Jesus even in scary situations.

Lesson 30

Biblical Character: Nehemiah
Scripture Text: Nehemiah 1-13
Memory Verse: Nehemiah 8:10
Lesson Outline:

- *Background* – Nehemiah was a Jew in exile in Babylon. He heard from a brother that Jews in Jerusalem were in trouble. The city wall was broken down and the gates burned, so people living there had no protection. This made Nehemiah very sad, so he prayed to God for an answer.
- *Story* – Nehemiah was the king's cupbearer. When he brought wine to the king, he looked very sad and the king noticed. The king asked him what the matter was. Even though Nehemiah was scared, he answered the king truthfully, told him his home city's trouble. The king asked what he needed to make it better, and Nehemiah asked if he could go and rebuild the city walls. He also asked for letters to give to governors he would pass on his way, and for a letter to use to get wood for the city gates. The King gave him all he needed, and let him go achieve his dream.
- *Main Achievement* - Nehemiah organized Jerusalem's people to rebuild the city walls.
- *Good/Bad Character Traits* – Nehemiah boldly dreamed of what he could do for God, and believed God to help him achieve it, no matter the obstacles.

Prayer Focus: Dreaming in God

- *Praise* – Thank you that you help us achieve our dreams.
- *Repent* – Forgive us we sometimes don't want to do what you ask us.
- *Ask for Others* – Help our church to be open to anything you want us to do for your Kingdom.
- *Ourselves* – Help us to be open to anything you ask us to do.

Lesson 31

Biblical Character: Ezra
Scripture Text: Nehemiah 8
Memory Verse: John 3:16
Lesson Outline:

- *Background* – Ezra was priest while Jerusalem was rebuilt. He worked with Nehemiah as a spiritual authority.
- *Story* – When the walls and the temple were repaired, people gathered to hear God's Word, asked Ezra to read it for them and explain. They made him a wooden pulpit, so they could see him. They stood as he opened the book. Ezra prayed to God and all the people said 'Amen' and raised their hands. They bowed their heads to the ground and worshipped God. The reading of the Law, and the explanations Ezra gave, so touched the people that they began to cry.
- *Main Achievement* - Ezra helped lead the rest of the Jews to bind together and rebuild the walls of Jerusalem.
- *Good/Bad Character Traits* – Ezra was a compassionate, strong leader.

Prayer Focus: Leadership

- *Praise* – Thank you for godly, inspired leadership.
- *Repent* – We're sorry we sometimes don't respect our parents, pastor, and teachers.
- *Ask for Others* – Strengthen our leadership to lead us according to your will.
- *Ourselves* – Help us respect and love our leaders.

Lesson 32

Biblical Characters: Elizabeth and Zechariah
Scripture Text: Luke 1
Memory Verse: Luke 1:42
Lesson Outline:

- *Background* – Elizabeth and Zechariah couldn't have children their whole lives, and now Elizabeth was past child-bearing age.
- *Story* – One day an angel told Zechariah Elizabeth would have a child, and to name him John. He didn't believe the angel, so the angel made Zechariah unable to talk until son's birth. While Elizabeth was pregnant, she saw her cousin Mary, and the baby inside of her moved, proving to her that Mary carried the Messiah. When the baby was born and dedicated to God, priests argued with Elizabeth over choosing John as a name, since it was not a family name. They asked Zechariah, and he wrote on a tablet the name was to be John. This showed his acceptance of God's plan, and he could talk again.
- *Main Achievement* - Elizabeth and Zechariah parented John the Baptist, who prepared people to receive Jesus.
- *Good/Bad Character Traits* – Bad: Zechariah had a little unbelief about God's promise. Good: they faithfully served God.

Prayer Focus: Waiting on God's Answer

- *Praise* – Thank you for providing answers to our prayers when the time is perfect.
- *Repent* – We are sorry for our impatience and frustration when we have to wait.
- *Ask for Others* – Give our church patience as we wait for answers to prayers.
- *Ourselves* – Help us praise you even when we don't have all the answers we want.

39

Lesson 33

Biblical Character: Mary and Joseph
Scripture Text: Luke 2
Memory Verse: Luke 2:14
Lesson Outline:

- *Background* – Mary and Joseph were young and engaged to be married.
- *Story* – One night an angel came to Mary and told her she would become pregnant by the Holy Spirit with the Messiah, Jesus. She became pregnant, and told Joseph. Joseph loved Mary, but couldn't believe she was still a virgin. He decided not to marry her, but not to publicly embarrass her. One night God spoke to him in a dream, telling him to marry Mary, because the baby came from God. Later, baby Jesus was born to this couple.
- *Main Achievement* - Mary and Joseph were the parents of the Messiah.
- *Good/Bad Character Traits* – They faithfully obeyed his voice.

Prayer Focus: Belief

- *Praise* – Thank you, Jesus, for helping us when we have a hard time believing promises you gave us.
- *Repent* – Forgive our unbelief and not understanding your plans.
- *Ask for Others* – Give our families strong belief in your promises.
- *Ourselves* – Let us willingly submit ourselves to your plan when you ask for our help.

Lesson 34

Biblical Character: Jesus
Scripture Text: Matthew 5-7
Memory Verse: Matthew 7:7-8
Lesson Outline:

- *Background* – Mary and Joseph were married, despite controversy Mary's pregnancy by the Holy Spirit caused.
- *Story* – Mary and Joseph had to travel to Bethlehem to pay taxes. Unfortunately, Mary soon had to have her baby, so the journey was very uncomfortable and hard. When they finally got to Bethlehem, all inns were filled up by travelers. A person took pity on them and let them rest in a stable. Baby Jesus was born that night.
- *Main Achievement* - He conquered hell and the grave by dying on the cross, allowing the whole human race to be saved.
- *Good/Bad Character Traits* – Jesus was the perfect, sinless human being. Everything he did was a good example for us.

Prayer Focus: Thankfulness

- *Praise* – Thank you Jesus for coming to this earth to save us and teach us.
- *Repent* – We're sorry people reject your gift of salvation.
- *Ask for Others* – Let our country's people's hearts open to receive salvation you offer.
- *Ourselves* – Let our hearts always thank you for your sacrifice on the cross.

Lesson 35

Biblical Character: John, the Baptist
Scripture Text: Luke 3
Memory Verse: Luke 3:4
Lesson Outline:

- *Background* – John was born to parents who could no longer have children. His birth was a miracle. He lived alone in the wilderness and dressed in animal skins. He ate locusts and wild honey.
- *Story* – John received God's Word in the wilderness. He moved to countryside near Jordan River and preached to people God's special message: baptism of repentance for the remission of sins. He told people a Messiah was coming, that they should prepare the Lord's way by getting their hearts right. He prophesied that one coming would baptize with the Holy Spirit and fire. Jesus came to be baptized by John in order to: fulfill all righteousness, be an example, and introduce himself to Israel as the Messiah. When Jesus was baptized, the Holy Spirit came down on him like a dove, proving to John he was indeed the Messiah. A voice also came from heaven, confirming to people his was God's chosen sacrifice.
- *Main Achievement* - John baptized many people in repentance, preparing them to receive Jesus' salvation.
- *Good/Bad Character Traits* – John faithfully served God even though his calling made him a social outcast and eventually cost him his life.

Prayer Focus: Repentance

- *Praise* – We praise you that you allow us to turn away from sins and follow you.
- *Repent* – We're sorry we sometimes choose to sin instead of to do your will.
- *Ask for Others* – Help people's hearts turn to you in repentance.
- *Ourselves* – Give us humble, repentant hearts that willingly serve you.

Lesson 36

REST

Lesson 37

Biblical Character: Matthew
Scripture Text: Matthew 9:9-13
Memory Verse: Matthew 19:26
Lesson Outline:

- *Background* – People hated Matthew because he collected taxes. Tax collectors were often dishonest and cheated people.
- *Story* – One day while Matthew was at work, Jesus passed by his place, stopped and told Matthew, 'Follow me.' Matthew immediately followed Jesus. Matthew took Jesus to his home, introduced him to all his sinner friends. When Pharisee's saw it, they asked why the Master ate with tax collectors and sinners. Jesus answered saying he had come to heal the sick, not healthy people. Jesus came to touch imperfect people, not those who thought they didn't need him.
- *Main Achievement* - Matthew recorded an eyewitness account of Jesus' ministry on earth.
- *Good/Bad Character Traits* – Bad: Matthew was a selfish man at first. Good: With God, Matthew changed.

Prayer Focus: Victory in Jesus

- *Praise* – Thank you for all things being possible with you.
- *Repent* – Forgive us for not trusting you when things look impossible.
- *Ask for Others* – Help our families always trust you when things get tough.
- *Ourselves* – Give us faith and desire to serve you even when it is difficult.

Lesson 38

Biblical Character: Nicodemus
Scripture Text: John 3:1-21
Memory Verse: John 3:5
Lesson Outline:

- *Background* – Nicodemus was very religious and a good man, but scared to come to Jesus in daytime when his friends would see him, so he came at night.
- *Story* – Nicodemus found Jesus, told him he believed Jesus was sent by God. Jesus said he must be born again. Nicodemus didn't understand—how could a man crawl back into his mother and be born again? Jesus told him he needed to be born of water and Spirit or he would never enter God's Kingdom. We were born of flesh the first time, but now we must experience spiritual birth.
- *Main Achievement* - Nicodemus received Jesus' testimony, even though it was unpopular.
- *Good/Bad Character Traits* – Bad: Nicodemus was scared to be seen talking with Jesus. Good: He was sensitive to God and desired a relationship with Jesus.

Prayer Focus: Sinners coming to Jesus

- *Praise* – Thank you that you have all answers this world's people need.
- *Repent* – We are sorry we don't always have a heart to witness like you want us to.
- *Ask for Others* – Put questions in hungry souls' hearts that can only be answered by God's Word.
- *Ourselves* – Make us lights of your love, so people will want to be saved by Jesus.

Lesson 39

Biblical Character: Mary and Martha of Bethany
Scripture Text: Luke 10:38-42
Memory Verse: John 4:24
Lesson Outline:

- *Background* – Mary and Martha were sisters and lived together.
- *Story* – One day Jesus visited. Mary chose to sit at Jesus' feet and listen. Martha was so worried about serving Jesus perfectly that she didn't sit to listen to him. She got upset with Mary and asked Jesus if he cared that Mary wasn't doing her part in serving. He answered by saying that Martha was troubled about many things, but that Mary was concerned only about listening and learning, which was the 'good' thing. He told Martha not to take that from Mary.
- *Main Achievement* - Mary and Martha extended hospitality to the Lord Jesus.
- *Good/Bad Character Traits* – Mary and Martha both had servant's hearts, but they expressed it differently; Mary worshipped through listening, and Martha worshipped through serving.

Prayer Focus: Forgiveness

- *Praise* – Thank you Jesus for forgiving our sins.
- *Repent* – We're sorry we sometimes don't appreciate your love.
- *Ask for Others* – Let our community's hurting, wounded people find love and forgiveness in our church.
- *Ourselves* – Give us loving, not proud and condemning, attitudes towards sinners.

Lesson 40

Biblical Character: Lazarus
Scripture Text: John 11
Memory Verse: John 11:4
Lesson Outline:

- *Background* – Lazarus was Mary's and Martha's brother.
- *Story* – Lazarus was very sick, so his sisters who worried about him and called Jesus to come and heal him. Jesus loved them, but still didn't start to come for 2 whole days, then called his disciples to come with him to raise Lazarus from the dead. By the time he got there, Lazarus had been dead 4 days and was already in the grave. Mary and Martha were so upset that Lazarus had died already when Jesus got there, because they knew if Jesus had been there he could have healed Lazarus. Jesus was so sad that he cried. Next, he went to the grave, ordered the stone rolled away, and called Lazarus to come out. Lazarus was raised from the dead and came out still wrapped in the grave clothes.
- *Main Achievement* - Lazarus was resurrected by Jesus himself.
- *Good/Bad Character Traits* – Lazarus was such a good man that the Bible says Jesus loved him.

Prayer Focus: God's miracles

- *Praise* – Thank you, Lord, that you're so powerful you can raise people from the dead.
- *Repent* – Forgive us for sometimes not trusting you to work out every situation.
- *Ask for Others* – Let your miracles witness to unbelievers.
- *Ourselves* – Use us to work miracles.

Lesson 41

Biblical Character: The Man at the Pool
Scripture Text: John 5
Memory Verse: James 5:15
Lesson Outline:

- *Background* – Many people waited by the same pool because there was an angel that would come and touch the waters every so often. The first person to make it to the pool after the angel touched it would be healed. One man had lain by Bethesda pool 38 years.
- *Story* – Jesus came by the water and saw the man there. He asked him if he wanted to be healed. The man said yes, but that he had no one to take him to the water when the angel came. People would step over him and get there first. Jesus told him to get up and walk, and immediately the man was whole.
- *Main Achievement* - He had faith for Jesus to heal him.
- *Good/Bad Character Traits* – He had great endurance and perseverance to sit up the same pool 38 years.

Prayer Focus: Healing

- *Praise* – Thank you, Jesus, for having power to heal us.
- *Repent* – We're sorry we sometimes don't trust you to heal our sickness.
- *Ask for Others* – Use healing to witness to our community's unbelievers.
- *Ourselves* – Give us boldness to pray for other people's healing.

Lesson 42

Biblical Character: Luke
Scripture Text: Luke 7
Memory Verse: Luke 6:27
Lesson Outline:
- *Background* – Luke wrote two books in the New Testament. He was an educated man and a doctor. He traveled with Paul on part of Paul's missionary trips. He was a faithful friend and soul-winner. In his biography of Jesus, he presents Jesus as the divine human, both God and man.
- *Story* – One day Jesus traveled to Capernaum, where a military man had a sick servant. People asked Jesus to come and heal him. When Jesus got near the house, the military man came out and stopped him, asked Jesus to simply say the word, and he believed his servant could be healed. Jesus was amazed at his faith, and the servant was healed when they reached home.
- *Main Achievement* – Luke wrote the third gospel and also the Book of Acts, recording Jesus' ministry and the Early Church.
- *Good/Bad Character Traits* – Luke faithfully served God, even when the times got tough during ministry.

Prayer Focus: Love
- *Praise* – We praise you, God, for loving us enough to die for our sins.
- *Repent* – Forgive us for not always showing your love to others, especially to people who aren't nice to us.
- *Ask for Others* – Help our church's people to love and understand people who persecute them.
- *Ourselves* – Give us love inside that makes us love and do good things for enemies.

Lesson 43

Biblical Character: Judas
Scripture Text: Matthew 26
Memory Verse: Matthew 26: 41
Lesson Outline:

*   *Background* – Judas, one of the original disciples, walked with Jesus 3 years.
*   *Story* – Judas was greedy for money and saw a chance to betray Jesus for a price. He went to the priests and they paid him 30 pieces of silver to take them to Jesus. Jesus knew this would happen, but he chose not to stop it, because he knew he had to die to save humanity. While Jesus prayed in the Garden of Gethsemane, Judas came with the chief priests, kissed Jesus to show the priests which one was the Master. They arrested him and took him to trial. Later, when Judas realized what he had done, he killed himself in shame.
*   *Main Achievement* - Judas showed the chief priests where Jesus was.
*   *Good/Bad Character Traits* – Judas had a greedy spirit that caused him to betray Jesus.

Prayer Focus: Unfaithfulness

*   *Praise* – Thank you that you can forgive any sin, even unfaithfulness.
*   *Repent* – We're sorry for when we've been unfaithful to you.
*   *Ask for Others* – Bring those who've been unfaithful to you back to your church.
*   *Ourselves* – Help us always be faithful to you, and, when we're not, to seek forgiveness instead of leaving church.

Lesson 44

Biblical Character: Pilate
Scripture Text: Matthew 27
Memory Verse: Matthew 27:37
Lesson Outline:

- *Background* – Pilate was a governor appointed by Caesar, head of the Roman Empire, in charge of keeping peace and punishing criminals.
- *Story* – Priests brought Jesus to the Romans to judge. All the Jews accused Jesus, but he didn't answer. Pilate finally judged him guilty, and brought him before the people. Pilate could release one criminal to the crowd in celebration of the feast. When he let the people choose between Jesus and a real criminal, the people told him to crucify Jesus and release the other man to them. Pilate knew that Jesus was innocent and felt bad about the decision, so he took water and washed his hands before the people, saying this made him innocent of Jesus' blood.
- *Main Achievement* - Pilate gave the decision to crucify Jesus.
- *Good/Bad Character Traits* – Pilate knew the difference between right and wrong, but was still influenced by evil people to kill Jesus.

Prayer Focus: God's will in the government

- *Praise* – Thank you that no one in our government can rule without your approval.
- *Repent* – We're sorry people in charge of our nation do not serve and honor you.
- *Ask for Others* – Give our government leaders wisdom and godly guidance so your will can be done in our nation.
- *Ourselves* – Give us a burden to pray for our government's leaders.

Lesson 45

Biblical Character: Thomas
Scripture Text: John 20
Memory Verse: John 20:29
Lesson Outline:

- *Background* – Thomas was one of Jesus' disciples.
- *Story* – After the crucifixion, the disciples were all very sad, because they thought Jesus had been killed forever. They felt very alone. Suddenly, Thomas heard from all his friends that they'd seen Jesus alive! He refused to believe and said he'd believe only if he saw Jesus and could put his finger where the nails had been and his hand into the side. Eight days later, Jesus came to him, and told him to look at and touch him. Thomas, amazed, confessed Jesus as Lord and God. Jesus told him those that came after him would believe without seeing and would be even more blessed.
- *Main Achievement* - He recognized Jesus as his Lord and God when he saw him.
- *Good/Bad Character Traits* – Bad: Thomas doubted Jesus. Good: He confessed truth and faithfully followed.

Prayer Focus: Patience of Jesus

- *Praise* – Thank you for being patient even when we don't believe.
- *Repent* – Forgive us when we don't believe in you completely.
- *Ask for Others* – Be patient, Jesus, with unbelievers and show them truth about who you are.
- *Ourselves* – When we have a hard time believing who you are, please be patient with us and give us faith.

Lesson 46

Biblical Character: James, the Lord's brother
Scripture Text: James 1-5, Acts 2
Memory Verse: James 4:10
Lesson Outline:

- *Background* – James was the half-brother of Jesus. His mother was Mary and his father was Joseph.
- *Story* – James grew up with Jesus like a normal brother. They had a relationship as siblings, but James had to receive Jesus as Savior as well. On Pentecost Day, James was in the upper room waiting for the Holy Spirit to come down on him. He was one of the 120 that received Spirit baptism. Later James wrote a book telling believers to be sincere and humble themselves before God. James had to learn that lesson with his half-brother Jesus before he could receive the Holy Spirit.
- *Main Achievement* - James wrote an epistle to the believers.
- *Good/Bad Character Traits* – James had a humble spirit and was a good teacher.

Prayer Focus: Humility

- *Praise* – Thank you for humbling yourself on the cross for our sins.
- *Repent* – Forgive us for our proud attitudes.
- *Ask for Others* – Let our church have humble attitudes towards God, so he will lift us up.
- *Ourselves* – Help us think of other people before we think of ourselves.

Lesson 47

Biblical Character: Peter
Scripture Text: Matthew 16:17-19, Acts 1-2
Memory Verse: Acts 2:38
Lesson Outline:

- *Background* – Peter was a fisherman when the Lord called him to be a disciple.
- *Story* –Jesus gave Peter a special promise—that he would have the Kingdom's keys. This means Peter would unlock salvation's gate. In Acts 2, we see this promise fulfilled. On Pentecost Day, Peter gets up to tell the crowd how to be saved: they are to repent, be baptized in Jesus' name, and receive the Holy Spirit. This promise is not just for people of that time, but for anyone in the future who would seek God.
- *Main Achievement* - Peter preached the most powerful message ever given for the first time: the salvation message.
- *Good/Bad Character Traits* – Bad: Peter denied the Lord before the crucifixion. Good: Peter after restoration was faithful to God.

Prayer Focus:

- *Praise* – Thank you for clearly providing salvation's plan in Acts.
- *Repent* – Forgive us for not spreading the gospel.
- *Ask for Others* – Open unsaved people's eyes so that they can come to full salvation.
- *Ourselves* – Give us a full understanding of what it means to repent, be baptized, and get filled with the Holy Spirit.

Lesson 48

Biblical Character: Mark
Scripture Text: Acts 12
Memory Verse: Mark 16:16
Lesson Outline:

- *Background* – Mark was an eyewitness of Jesus' miracles and teachings, and a friend of apostles Peter and Paul.
- *Story* – Christians were persecuted. Peter was arrested and put in jail. In Mark's home, the church prayed for Peter's release. While they prayed, God released Peter from prison and an angel led him out. He went to Mark's home and knocked at the door. When Rhoda heard his voice, she got so excited, she forgot to open the door. She ran to tell everyone Peter was there, and they didn't believe her. Finally, they heard the knocking and opened the door so Peter could come in.
- *Main Achievement* - Mark completed an eyewitness account of Jesus.
- *Good/Bad Character Traits* – Mark faithfully followed Jesus.

Prayer Focus: Salvation

- *Praise* – Thank you for letting us be saved through baptism.
- *Repent* – Forgive us for not always telling others about baptism in Jesus' Name.
- *Ask for Others* – Reveal through us to all people Jesus' Name baptism.
- *Ourselves* – Give us desire to spread the news about true baptism.

Lesson 49

Biblical Character: Stephen
Scripture Text: Acts 6-7
Memory Verse: John 7:55
Lesson Outline:
- *Background* – Stephen was one of the seven people chosen to help apostles. He was full of the Holy Spirit and of faith.
- *Story* - Stephen went to a synagogue to preach Jesus Christ, but teachers and leaders would not accept the good news. People hired false witnesses to speak against Stephen. Still, Stephen did not back down and defended the message courageously. Finally, people listening to him decided to kill him. Instead of fighting back or feeling fear, Stephen looked up to heaven and saw Jesus ready to receive him into heaven. When he told the crowd this, they got even more angry and killed him immediately.
- *Main Achievement* - Stephen was the first Christian martyr.
- *Good/Bad Character Traits* – Stephen bravely, boldly faced terrible persecution.

Prayer Focus: Sacrifice
- *Praise* – Thank you that you reward those who sacrifice their lives for your Kingdom.
- *Repent* – Forgive us when we're sometimes unwilling to sacrifice our lives for you.
- *Ask for Others* – Give our church desire to sacrifice all for you.
- *Ourselves* – Give us willingness to give you more of ourselves, so that more souls can come to salvation.

Lesson 50

Biblical Character: Paul
Scripture Text: Acts 9, 22
Memory Verse: Romans 12:1-2
Lesson Outline:

- *Background* – Paul was educated and dedicated. He lived life in obedience to the law. He persecuted Christians.
- *Story* – One day Paul was on the way to Damascus to kill some Christians, saw a light, fell onto the ground, and heard a voice ask, 'Why do you persecute me?' Paul asked who was speaking. The voice answered, 'I am Jesus, who you persecute.' When Paul asked what he should do, Jesus told him to go to the city where his next step would be shown him. Paul was struck blind by the vision, so the men with him had to lead him to the city. In the city he met a man named Ananias who prayed for him. Paul received salvation, his sight, and his calling as an apostle at this time.
- *Main Achievement* - Paul made three missionary journeys and wrote much of the New Testament.
- *Good/Bad Character Traits* – Bad: Before he came to Jesus, Paul was proud. Good: After he came to God, he learned to be humble.

Prayer Focus: God's guidance

- *Praise* – Thank you for caring enough about us to stop us and enable us to serve you.
- *Repent* – We're sorry we sometimes don't follow your instructions.
- *Ask for Others* – Give more sinners their own "Damascus Road" experience where they come in contact with the true God.
- *Ourselves* – Help us always open to your guidance and direction for our lives.

Lesson 51

Biblical Character: The Apostle John
Scripture Text: Revelation 1-22
Memory Verse: Revelation 3:20
Lesson Outline:
- *Background* – John was the Zebedee's son and James' younger brother. He and his brother were called 'Sons of Thunder.' Later, he called himself 'the disciple Jesus loved.'
- *Story* – John lived in Jerusalem until A.D. 70, when a terrible war destroyed the city. Then he went to Asia Minor and led the church in Ephesus for 25 years. He was then put into exile on the Patmos Island because of his stand for Jesus. While he lived on that island, God inspired him to write Revelation, which tells us what will happen in the last days before Jesus returns.
- *Main Achievement* - John wrote several New Testament books, including the Gospel of John, the 3 Epistles of John, and Revelation.
- *Good/Bad Character Traits* – Bad: John had an anger problem at his ministry's beginning. Good: He allowed God to change him into a better person.

Prayer Focus: Jesus' Second Coming
- *Praise* – Thank you that you're coming back soon to take us to Heaven.
- *Repent* – We're sorry we sometimes forget how soon your coming is and we don't witness as we should.
- *Ask for Others* – Give our church urgency about how little time we have left to win our communities.
- *Ourselves* – Help us to make sure that we're ready for your second coming.

Lesson 52

REST

Stanley Scism writes books, articles, college lectures, songs, poems and other things he might have forgotten just now. He founded, presides over and teaches occasionally in Scism Christian University's campuses. He founded and leads Yesu Mandali in Nepal, Yesu Kalishia in India, and Stanley Society in India. He founded Wonderful Words publishing, Light and Life music ministry, Head & Heart Ministers' Meetings. He enjoys his friends in the USA, UK, Republic of Ireland, India, Nepal and in nations he doesn't get to visit regularly. He wants you to come to saving faith in Jesus Christ, to be baptized in Jesus name, and to be filled with the Spirit of Jesus.

His books are, in order of publication:

Lera, a biography of a minister from Manipur, who also lived many years in Meghalaya, who baptized over 6000 people, started over 50 churches, opened up three whole new areas to the message.

Little Lady, a biography of a lady from Arunachal Pradesh, who endured horrible privations as a child, found relief and rescue in Jesus Christ, has told many of her home people about Him.

Northwest Passage, volume one of the biography of Ellis Scism, who grew up in Oregon, went to college in California, pastored churches in Washington and Idaho, led a group of ministers from Alaska to Wyoming—all this before going to India as a founding missionary.

A Look at Revelation, James Stewart's teaching on the Biblical book, rendered into writing by Stanley Scism

Baptism, a pocket-sized study.

Tell Me About Your Life!, Katy Collins (mostly) and Stanley Scism (some) wrote these Sunday school lessons for children.

Stanley Scism's Songs!, his lyrics to his and other people's melodies.

Devoted, sixty short meditations for public or personal devotions.

A Look at Spiritual Gifts, James Stewart's teaching on gifts of the Spirit, rendered into writing by Stanley Scism.

A Himalayan Christmas, a drama of the year's highest point, set in the world's highest place.

Praying Heart, 13 meditations on devotion and communion for one quarter of the year.

Big Blue Songbook: Sigma Songbook, 9th edition. Compiled by Stanley Scism for SCI-New Delhi.

Do You Hear What I Hear?. Christmas songs compiled by Stanley Scism for SCI-New Delhi.

Katy Collins was born in Joplin, MO and attended the University of Arkansas in Fayetteville, AR. She received a Bachelor of Science in Elementary Education with an endorsement in Teaching English as a Second Language, as well as a Master of Arts in Teaching. After graduation in 2005, she worked as an Associate in Missions in Mexico City, Mexico and New Delhi, India. During her time in India, she taught 3 classes at Scism Christian Institute: Teaching Home Bible Studies, Survey of Scriptures, and Youth Ministry. She also taught Sunday School in a local church and home Bible studies in a house church.

While she was in Delhi, Bro. and Sis. Tim Pedigo from Indianapolis, IN came to teach at the Bible College for a week and told her about Calvary Christian School (CCS), a ministry of Calvary Tabernacle in Indianapolis. Through that contact, Katy came to teach at CCS in 2006. She teaches third grade and is also one of the teachers in the Young Adult Sunday School class at Calvary Tabernacle.

Katy wrote these Sunday School lessons during her time in India. They are published with hope they will be of use in children's ministry in the part of the world she came to love so much. The lessons are dedicated to men and women who work tirelessly teaching children God's Word. They come to you covered in prayer for teachers who will use them and the people to whom they will minister.